The Scots of Montreal

Tobacco store figure
(42nd Highlander taking snuff.)
Wood carving, 108 cm. × 30 cm.
Circa 1825. McCord Museum, M995.44

The Scots of Montreal

A Pictorial Album

Edited by

Nancy Marrelli and Simon Dardick

Véhicule Press

Véhicule Press in collaboration with
the McCord Museum of Canadian History and the St. Andrew's Society of Montreal

Published with the generous assistance of the McCord Museum of Canadian History, the St. Andrew's Society of Montreal, the Book Publishing Industry Development Program of the Department of Canadian Heritage, and the Société de développement des entreprises culturelles du Québec (SODEC).

The Scots of Montreal is based on the McCord Museum exhibition, *The Scots: Dyed-in-the-Wool Montrealers / Les Écossais: les Montréalais pure laine*. This book could not have been realized without the efforts of Moira McCaffrey, Director of Exhibitions and Research, McCord Museum; exhibition researcher Heather McNabb; interpretive planner Pierre Wilson; Marilyn Aitken, McCord staff photographer; Stéphanie Poisson, rights and reproductions technician; Melanie Martens, publications officer and all who worked on the exhibition. Mary Johnston Cox, historian of the St. Andrew's Society provided valuable fact checking. The publisher and editors particularly want to thank Dr. Victoria Dickenson, executive director of the McCord Museum, Ian Aitken, president of the St. Andrew's Society of Montreal, who suggested the book, and Bruce McNiven, first vice-president of the St. Andrew's Society of Montreal, who also provided assistance.

Cover and interior design: J.W. Stewart
Cover image: Master Hugh Allan, 1867. Painted photograph. Photograph by William Notman, watercolour by John Arthur Fraser. Gift of Mrs. Gertrude H. Bourne, McCord Museum, N-1981.16.1
Back cover and frontispiece: Tobacco store figure (42nd Highlander taking snuff.) Wood carving, 108 cm. × 30 cm., circa 1825. McCord Museum, M995.44.
Printed by AGMV-Marquis Inc.

Library and Archives Canada Cataloguing in Publication

The Scots of Montreal : a pictorial album / edited by Nancy Marrelli and Simon Dardick.

Includes index.
ISBN 1-55065-192-7

1. Scottish Canadians—Québec (Province)—Montréal—History.
2. Scots—Québec (Province)—Montréal—History. 3. Scottish Canadians—
Québec (Province)—Montréal—Biography. 4. Montréal (Québec)—History.
5. Montréal (Québec)—Biography. I. Marrelli, Nancy II. Dardick, Simon, 1943-

FC2947.9.S3S38 2004   971.4'280049163   C2004-904016-2

Véhicule Press   —   www.vehiculepress.com

Canadian distribution — LitDistCo Distribution, 100 Armstrong Avenue, Georgetown, Ontario L7G 5S4
800.591.6250 / orders@litdistco.ca
U.S. distribution — Independent Publishers Group, 814 North Franklin Street, Chicago, IL 60610
800.888.4741 / orders@ipgbook.com
Printed and bound in Canada

Table of Contents

"Go into whatever country you will, you will always find Scotchmen.
They penetrate into every climate: you meet them in all the various departments
of travellers, soldiers, merchants, adventurers, domestics. Consult the history of their own nation
from the earliest period, and that of other nations, and you will find that if any dangerous and difficult
enterprise has been undertaken, any uncommon proofs given of patience or activity,
any new countries visited and improved, that a Scotchman
has borne some share in the performance."

— Edward Topham, 1775

Preface

I am a self-confessed Scot-o-phile — the evidence: my hobby is Highland dancing and I happen to have married a bagpiper. In my twenty years working as researcher and cataloguer in the McCord Museum's Notman Photographic Archives I have encountered countless examples of successful Montreal Scots, and for my own graduate research I chose to explore the working-class Scottish experience in this great city. For this reason, it was a dream come true to participate in the research and development of the McCord exhibition *The Scots: Dyed-in-the-Wool Montrealers*, a project that eventually led to this book.

The skills and efforts of many individuals are needed to bring an exhibition to fruition. In this case, the curatorial committee included McCord Executive Director Victoria Dickenson; Moira McCaffrey, the McCord's Director of Exhibitions and Research; Peter Rider, Atlantic Provinces Historian with the Canadian Museum of Civilization; and museological consultant Pierre Wilson. After initial ideas were proposed, one of the first tasks was to establish the Scottish content within the McCord's collections. This meant scrolling through the Museum database as well as consulting with curators and others familiar with the collections. We also searched other institutions for objects that would complement those of the McCord. We soon found, however, as we had suspected, that the McCord Museum was the repository for a large amount of wonderful Scots-related material.

Another important step in the exhibition's development was a search for written material available on the subject of the Scots in Montreal. As we did not find a great deal already in print, we chose to consult with scholars by holding a colloquium, held at the McCord in Montreal in May of 2002 in collaboration with the McGill University History Department. Speakers addressed a wide variety of topics and discussed the proposed themes of the exhibition during a lively interactive session.

The goal of the exhibition from the outset was to inform, educate, and interest people in the fascinating story of the Scots in Montreal, and to shine a brighter light on their incomparable contributions to the 19th century development of Montreal and, by extension, Canada. Scottish intellectual and philanthropic endeavours were emphasized to add to the already well-known commercial success stories, and to suggest some possible reasons why they did so well for themselves here.

So many Scottish "characters" stand out in Montreal's history, it was at times difficult to choose who deserved precious space in the 4,000 square foot exhibition. Inevitably, some very interesting people were excluded. At times we also had a wealth of objects illustrating one theme or idea, and were forced to eliminate some real treasures. Nevertheless, certain aspects of the story were harder to bring to life due to absences in the collections, a problem we overcame by borrowing from other institutions and individuals. These collaborations added enormously to the show. A portion of a stained glass window from the Church of St. Andrew and St. Paul, for example, was a beautiful evocation of the Montreal Scots' religious heritage. We were especially pleased to include this object since the Church's 200th anniversary (celebrated in 2003) served as a catalyst for the exhibition.

In spite of all our best efforts, there remained a few subjects for which artifacts were unavailable; in these cases, text would have to suffice. The stories of Scottish women, and of poorer, less successful Scots are both difficult to represent in material terms, as their belongings tend to have been lost to the historical record. This is due in part to the preferences and prejudices of previous collectors. Since many museum artifacts were originally collected precisely because they were property of the more prominent members of society, the difficulty in finding traces of the poor Scottish nanny, cabinetmaker or unemployed labourer is understandable. But the problem was also practical: It would have been difficult to obtain significant objects from poorer immigrants who out of necessity used, reused, and recycled their belongings until they were worn out, broken or beyond use. Many people would dearly love to have something as simple as the plaid of a soldier from the Fraser Highlanders who settled in Quebec—unfortunately, such an item does not exist. James Thompson himself declared how happy he was to be rid of the troublesome garment when he left his soldier's life behind. A Highland soldier's plaid may have ended its days as scraps in a rug, or filling cracks between logs in a settler's wooden home. Museums today may be poorer for it, but at least they have written accounts like that of James Thompson, which also greatly enriched our exhibition.

It is a tremendous pleasure that following the exhibition *The Scots: Dyed-in-the-Wool Montrealers* has come a further project to create this beautiful book, thanks to the collaboration of the McCord Museum, the Saint Andrew's Society and Véhicule Press.

Heather McNabb
McCord Museum of Canadian History
Montreal, Quebec, May 2005

Beginning in the 18th and throughout the 19th century,
Montrealers of Scottish origin governed business, finance, industry and transportation in the city.
They also influenced the development of educational, scientific and political institutions,
and in many cases bequeathed property and even enormous fortunes
for the lasting benefit of their fellow citizens.

The Scots—many of them of humble origin—were successful in Montreal.
They were in the right place at the right time with the right combination of education, religious morals, a
strict work ethic, personal ambition and, not least, the vision to see Montreal as the future
Canadian metropolis. Looking beyond the stern official portraits and preconceptions
we discover how deeply the Scottish thistle is rooted in Montreal's soil.

The Scots Arrive

For years, the British had been trying to wrest control over New France from the French army, fighting from one fort to the next with limited success. When General Amherst took Louisbourg in 1758, the tide turned in the redcoats' favour. Quebec fell one year later on the Plains of Abraham. By September 6, 1760, Amherst and Murray's troops had their guns trained on Montreal. This time the British wouldn't have to fight, for with 17,000 armed men they outnumbered the 2,500 French soldiers almost 7 to 1. On September 8, the city gates were thrown open and the troops marched in. Great Britain peacefully took possession of the last remaining bastion of New France.

The Scottish soldiers in the 78th Fraser Highlanders acquitted themselves brilliantly in this long campaign, on the Plains of Abraham and in many other battles. After the regiment was disbanded in 1763, many of its soldiers decided to stay on in Canada.

Scottish roots had been planted in Canadian soil.

33. BATTLE OF QUEBEC. GENERAL FRASER LEADING HIS HIGHLANDERS. 1759.

Battle of Quebec. General Fraser Leading His Highlanders in 1759.
Coloured ink on mercerized cotton, mid-20th century.

Gift of Mrs. M. Easton, McCord Museum, M975.172.1.30

A number of the soldiers and officers from the 78th Fraser Highlanders settled in Lower Canada after their Regiment disbanded. The wealthiest among them, mostly officers, purchased or were given seigneuries. Of the 43 seigneuries that passed into British hands from 1760 to 1791, 27 went to Scots. But not only Fraser Highlanders would settle in Canada. Many Scots came to seek a new life and opportunities in the colonies, including some who were forced to leave their homeland.

The final defeat of the partisan Scottish Jacobites at Culloden in April 1746 and the subsequent banning of certain Scottish customs by the British Government weakened the ties that had bound the clan chiefs and their communities. This turn of events could have encouraged the poorer clan members, by freeing them of the sometimes-excessive authority of the clan chiefs and allowing them to own the land they and their ancestors had farmed as tenants. In fact, the opposite occurred. The clan chiefs, crippled by debt and unable to invest in new farming technology, rented out their land for the raising of sheep and cattle, which required little labour. As a result, the tenant families were removed from the land — often by force — and summarily shipped off to the colonies. The eviction of tens of thousands of Highlanders, known as the Clearances, was one of the most painful episodes in Scottish history.

Some Scots left cities like Glasgow to escape poverty, and others left the Highlands or the Lowlands forcefully or voluntarily. Some were part of a clan or a family group, or emigrated with friends or with a kist, or trunk, as their only companion. Scottish emigrants all shared the same dream: to better their lives. Some left for Canada, Australia, New Zealand, South Africa, India or Hong Kong, while others went to the United States, Argentina, Poland, Russia and other parts of the world. Canada offered opportunities for land ownership and social advancement that were no longer available in the mother country.

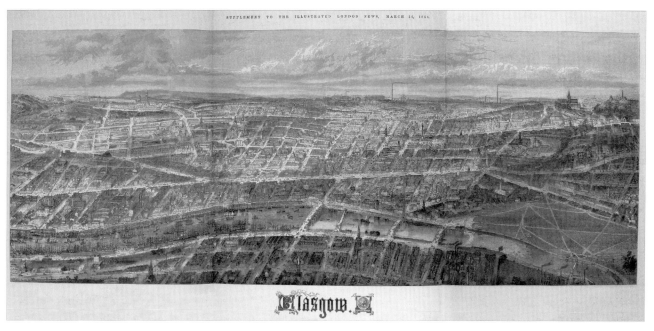

Glasgow.
Illustrated London News, March 26, 1864. Engraving by Charles Sulmandel.

Gift of David Ross McCord, McCord Museum, M14599

In the early 19th century, the ocean crossing from Scotland to Canada took 38 days on average. Scottish emigrants had to provide for themselves on the perilous voyage. Each one was to bring "oatmeal and potatoes as staple articles; say eight packs of the former, and fifteen or twenty stones [a stone is 6.35 kg or 14 pounds] of the latter; also eight or ten pounds of salt herrings, a few pounds of treacle, a piece of good bacon, about twenty of sea biscuits, with cheese and butter as convenient." (W. G. Mack, *Recommendations to Travellers*, 1837)

Conditions on board ship were deplorable, so much so that that the weakest passengers didn't survive the journey. "To descend on an empty stomach into steerage No.1 was an adventure that required some nerve. The stench was atrocious; each respiration tasted in the throat like some horrible kind of cheese ..." (R. L. Stevenson, 1879).

The advent of steamships cut the time at sea considerably, so that by the late 19th century the Atlantic crossing took only six days. As with most immigrant groups, Scottish benevolent societies, churches and other social groups helped ease the way for new arrivals and created a bit of home for Montrealers of Scottish origin.

Dear sister,
After a somewhat long and rather stormy voyage, by the good providence of Almighty God I arrived safe and well in this city, just seven weeks after parting with so many kind, dear friends at Aberdeen ... we stood mostly by farmers and farm labourers. There were four or five blacksmiths three bakers half a dozen wrights and joiners and a tailor who might almost be said to have crossed the Atlantic on his goose and needle as he sewed all the time unless the rolling of the ship turned him off his chest lid. We had also two fiddlers and a poet.

– Excerpt from a letter from James Thomson to his sister, July 18, 1844, Montreal.
Upon his arrival in Montreal, Thomson became an assistant in McDougall's Bakery, on Wellington Street.

1332-HARBOR FROM CUSTOM HOUSE MONTREAL

View of the Harbour, Montreal, 1884.
Photograph by William Notman & Son.

Purchase from Associated Screen News Ltd., McCord Museum, VIEW-1332

Coming Together

What the newcomers had in common was a tendency to settle among,
and to fraternize with, their fellow Scots — whether in town or countryside — combined with
a strong commitment to the creation of Scottish institutions within their community.

—J.M. Bumsted, *The Scots in Canada*

People of French, English, Irish, Scottish and other origins rubbed shoulders and worked side by side every day in 19th century Montreal. There were Roman Catholics, Anglicans, Presbyterians and many other religious groups in the city. Much of the time, people from these diverse cultures got along very well despite their different origins and beliefs. Yet each group felt the need to rally together under its own banner, to stick together and to assert its particular ethnic or religious affiliations.

Things were particularly tense in Montreal in the 1830s. Political disputes between the *Patriotes* and the Tories divided the population along ethnic lines. In 1834 alone, the French Canadians founded the Saint-Jean-Baptiste society, the Irish, the St. Patrick's Society and the English, the St. George's Society. These societies were initially intended to rally their members politically under ethnic and partisan banners. They all pursued the same goals for the group they served and they soon also provided support for their own members in times of necessity, and worked for the benefit of other needy people within their own ethnic communities.

The St. Andrew's Society of Montreal was founded in 1835 by a group of Scots as a charitable organization to provide aid to the growing number of Scottish immigrants arriving in Montreal. Its first president was businessman Peter McGill. Through its history the Society has offered assistance, advice, and scholarships to people of Scottish ancestry, and it has promoted activities that celebrate and preserve Scottish traditions and customs. Its early motto was "Relieve the Distressed." The motto later became "Nemo me impune lacessit" (No one provokes me with impunity), the motto of Scotland.

The Society also organized traditional celebrations and social events that promoted Scottish pride and identity. In 1929 members donated money that was used to erect a statue to Scotland's most beloved poet, Robert Burns (1759-96). The statue was erected in 1930 and it still stands in Dominion Square, now renamed Dorchester Square.

"Relieve the distressed"
Motto of the St. Andrew's Society of Montreal, late 19th century.
Engraving by John Henry Walker (1831-99).

Gift of David Ross McCord, McCord Museum, M930.50.1.670

In 1856 the St. Andrew's Society of Montreal established a temporary home on Hermine Street where they could provide short-term refuge for Scots in distress, particularly newly arrived immigrants. Within a few months the Society leased property on St. George Street and the first St. Andrew's Home was established to provide shelter for those in need. In 1866 the Society purchased a property at Dorchester (now René-Lévesque) and St-Urbain in which they set up the second St. Andrew's Home. The facility served new arrivals needing help as well as the local population who were destitute or needed shelter because of illness. By 1887 they had outgrown the old site and a new property at 403 Aqueduct Street was bought and outfitted; this property included facilities for the Scottish Choir, a Sunday School, and the Caledonian Society.

By the 1920s Scottish immigration had decreased, other agencies had assumed responsibility for immigration, and in 1925, to the regret of many Montreal Scots, the Society sold the Home and property to the Ernest Cousins Ltd. dairy. The proceeds of the sale were set aside to be used by the Society to care for those in need.

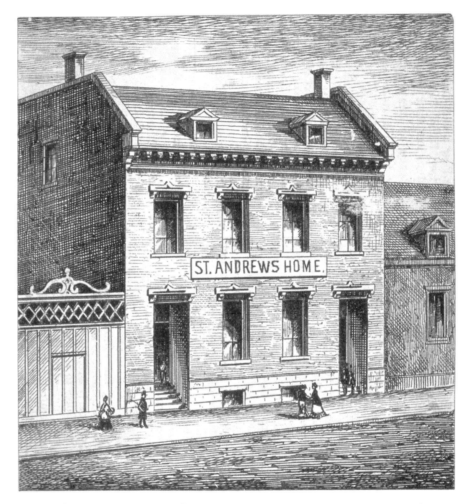

St. Andrew's Home on Dorchester Street (now René-Lévesque) at St-Urbain.
Canadian Illustrated News, August 21, 1875.

During the 1830s, the numbers of Scottish immigrants arriving in Montreal increased greatly. The St. Andrew's Society of Montreal stepped in to help the neediest newcomers get settled or continue their journey to their final destination. Even if there were no friends or family at the wharf to greet an arriving Scot, the benevolent society was there.

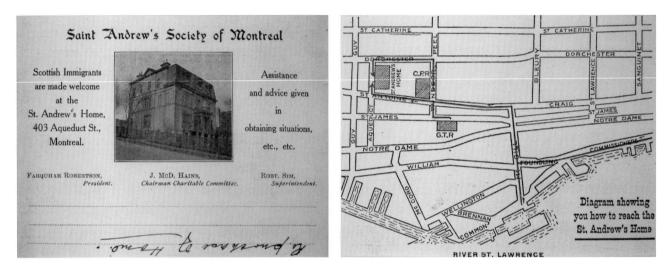

Handout given to Scottish immigrants as they stepped ashore in Montreal
with directions to the St. Andrew's Home on Aqueduct Street,
where they could get temporary shelter, circa 1914.

St. Andrew's Society of Montreal Archives

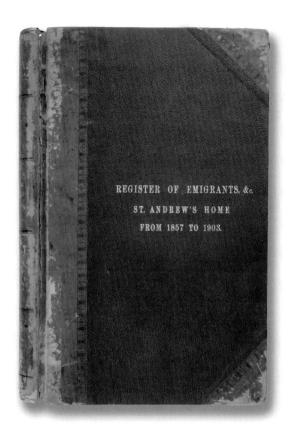
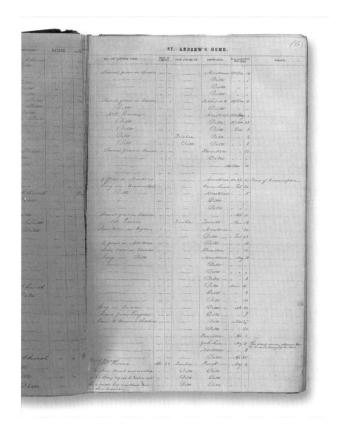

Register of emigrants at the St. Andrew's Home, 1857-1903.

St. Andrew's Society of Montreal Archives

From its beginning in 1835, the St. Andrew's Society held an annual dinner for members and invited guests. On November 30, 1848, instead of the dinner, the Society organized a Caledonia Assembly. Between 1849 and 1854 the annual dinners resumed. After a constitutional change, the dinners were replaced in 1855 by concerts or soirées. The St. Andrew's Society organized its first St. Andrew's Ball on November 30, 1871. By the late 1870s, the St. Andrew's Ball had become an eagerly anticipated annual event, attended by the Scottish elite and other well-connected Montrealers. The balls have continued as an annual tradition, cancelled only in times of adversity or when replaced by another event.

St. Andrew's Society of Montreal ball at the Windsor Hotel in 1878.
Composite photograph by Notman & Sandham, 1879.

Purchase from Associated Screen News Ltd., McCord Museum, II-51688

The Caledonian Society was originally formed in 1855 as an adjunct to the St. Andrew's Society, to encourage sports, cultural and social activities. The Society took its name from Caledonia, the name given by the Romans to the lands the Scots would settle in the sixth century.

(*left*, *above*) The Caledonia Games, Decker Park, August 15, 1872.
Sketch of the dancing of the Ghillie Callum. *Canadian Illustrated News*, August 24, 1872.
Gift of Charles deVolpi, McCord Museum, M975.62.241

(*right*, *above*) Emblem of the Caledonian Society of Montreal. Engraving by John Henry Walker (1831-99).
Gift of David Ross McCord, McCord Museum, M930.50.1.643

Past presidents of the Caledonian Society of Montreal.
Composite photograph by Summerhayes & Walford, 1889.

Gift of David Miller, McCord Museum, MP-1978.199

Sports were popular entertainment in Montreal in all seasons. Sports and sports clubs were an important part of the Scots community; club members participated not only in sports activities but also social events and community gatherings. In 1807 a group of Scots founded the Montreal Curling Club, later called the Royal Montreal Curling Club. It is the oldest curling club in North America and the oldest sport club in continuous operation in Canada. Curling became popular with the ladies too.

Lachine Ladies Curling Club, 1903. Photograph by William Notman & Son.
Purchase from Associated Screen News Ltd., McCord Museum, II-147881

A curling match at the foot of Jacques Cartier Square. *Illustrated London News*, February 17, 1855.

Photograph of the engraving. Gift of Stanley G. Triggs, McCord Museum, MP-0000.817.6.

The debate still rages whether golf was a Dutch or a Scottish invention, but there is no denying that Scotland is the chosen Home of Golf. The first written mention of it appeared in Scotland in 1457. From the mid-15th century golf was a favourite amusement of royalty, nobility and the most humble Scots, with little distinction of rank. The Golfing Societies formed in the mid-18th century established private courses and exclusive Club Houses, although the prescriptive right to play on links or courses in Scotland is maintained to this day for local inhabitants. For the affluent and privileged members of the golfing societies golf also became the opportunity to talk business and to dine sumptuously. So it comes as no surprise that the first golf club in North America was founded on November 4, 1873, in Canada's metropolis, where Canadian barons of trade lived — many of them of Scottish birth or ancestry.

It took a year's work to ready the site of the Royal Montreal Golf Club, on either side of Park Avenue on the eastern slope of Montreal's mountain. By 1874, members could meet on Wednesdays and Saturdays at Fletcher's Field (now Jeanne-Mance Park), for nine holes of golf.

The Royal Montreal Golf Club is still active today and is situated on Ile Bizard.

Senator Sir George Drummond with golf club, Montreal, QC, 1900.
Photograph by William Notman & Son.

Purchase from Associated Screen News Ltd., McCord Museum, II-136465

Key.   Royal Montreal Golf Club. 1882.

1   F. Wolferstan Thomas.   13   W. M. Ramsay.   25   Mr Young.   Quebec
2   Miss K. Esdaile.   14   John Hope.   26   John Porteous.   do.
3   Mrs. Esdaile.   15   Alex. Stoddart   Liverpool E.   27   Josh. C. Collins.
4   Miss Geraldine Esdaile.   16   Chas. G. Sidey.   28   Homer Taylor.
5   Mrs. Chapl. John Taylor.   17   Park Ranger.   29   Rev. R. C. Campbell.
6   John T. Redpath.   18   Gilbert Scott.   30   Eric Mann.
7   Mrs. Dr. Daynes.   19   Mr. Dennistoun.   31   Mr R. Esdaile.
8   Dr. Daynes.   20   Alex. Dennistoun.   32   Hanbury L. McDougall.
9   J. K. Oswald.   21   Geo. A. Drummond.   33   Rev. Canon Ellegood.
10 Z. S. Greenshields.   22   John Taylor. Capt.   34   C. C. Foster.
11 John S. McLennan.   23   Rob. M. Esdaile.   35   W. R. Elmenhorst.
12 John G. Sidey.   24   D. D. Sidey.   36   Jas. Stewart.   Herald.
                                                               37   Chas. Stimson.

Royal Montreal Golf Club. Composite photograph by Notman & Sandham, 1882.

Purchase from Associated Screen News Ltd., McCord Museum, VIEW-18907

Julia Drummond and George Alexander Drummond
(later Lady Drummond and Sir George Alexander Drummond)

Members of the Montreal Scots community were active in many different organizations.
Montreal-born of Scots ancestry, Julia Drummond (Grace Julia Parker, 1851-1942) was an early feminist. She was the widow of the Reverend George Hamilton when she married Senator George Alexander Drummond in 1884. Senator Drummond (knighted in 1904) had himself been widowed by the recent death of Helen Redpath.

Julia Drummond helped found and was active in a number of women's organizations. She was president of the Montreal section of the National Council of Women in 1893, and she laid the groundwork for the Charity Organization that was renamed the Family Welfare Association. She was a director of the Women's Canadian Historical Society and helped establish the Montreal branch of the Victorian Order of Nurses. As chair of the provincial committee for women's suffrage, she also fought to win the vote for women.

(left) Julia Drummond, later Lady Drummond, 1897. Oil on canvas by Robert Harris (1849-1919)

Gift of the Estate of Guy Drummond, McCord Museum, M988.98.2

(right) George Alexander Drummond, later Sir George Alexander Drummond, 1868.
Photograph by William Notman (1826-91).

Purchase from Associated Screen News Ltd., McCord Museum, I-35407

Political Life

"Were I not French, I would choose to be a Scot."

— Sir Wilfrid Laurier, 1893

In 1763, after distinguishing himself in the Seven Years' War, at Louisbourg, Quebec and Montreal, James Murray (born in Ballencrieff, Scotland in 1721, died in 1794) became the first Governor of the Province of Quebec. He said that the Canadians were "perhaps, the best and bravest Race on the Globe, a Race, that have already got the better of every National Antipathy to their Conquerors, and could they be indulged with a very few Privileges, which the Laws of England do not allow to Catholics at home, must in a very short Time become the most faithful & useful Set of Men in this American Empire."

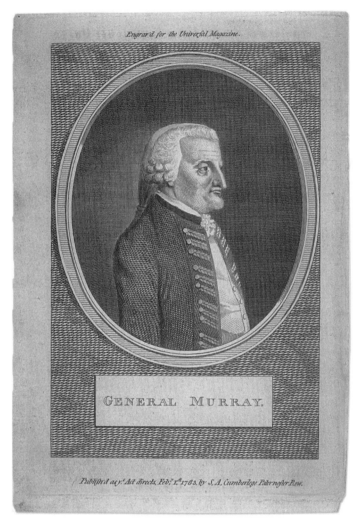

Engrav'd for the Universal Magazine.

GENERAL MURRAY.

Publish'd as y.e Act directs, Feb.y 1.st 1783. by S. A. Cumberlege Paternoster Row.

General James Murray.
Etching published by S. A. Cumberlege, February 1, 1783.

Gift of David Ross McCord, McCord Museum, M3436

The Fenians, named for an ancient group of Irish knights, were a revolutionary group of Irishmen dedicated to the overthrow of British rule in Ireland. During the American Civil War, the creation of Fenian regiments in the U.S. Federal Army was viewed as a potential threat to Canada. The Fenians led raids into Canada in the hopes of gaining control of Canada to hold it ransom in exchange for the freedom of Ireland.

A number of influential Scots businessmen in Montreal responded to this threat by forming the 5th Battalion Royal Light Infantry in 1862, which would become the Black Watch, or Royal Highland Regiment, of Canada.

It takes its name from the Black Watch of Scotland, independent Highland companies formed in the 18th century following the Jacobite uprisings to maintain order in the Highlands. Its modern colours and uniform are inspired by the Black Watch of Scotland as well. Since 1862 this Canadian regiment has taken part in major conflicts around the world, and today it is a modern infantry, providing trained soldiers to augment regular forces and aid civil authorities in times of crisis.

Black Watch Armoury, Bleury Street, Montreal, 1940-42.
Photograph, William Notman & Son.
Purchase from Associated Screen News Ltd., McCord Museum, VIEW-26216

The 5th Royal Highlanders returning from the Boer War, 1900.
Ink sketch by Henri Julien (1852-1908).

Gift of David Ross McCord, McCord Museum, M677

From the time the Act of Union in 1840 combined the assemblies of Upper and Lower Canada, Parliament was located in Kingston. However, the members wanted to be closer to the centres of decision-making, and to take advantage of various services, so in 1844 Parliament moved to Montreal, into the former St. Anne's Market building (1832) in Place d'Youville.

Political institutions in Canada were paralyzed in the early 1840s. The Union Parliament was unable to govern the country, given the refusal by the Governor and his clique to relinquish the reins of power. But things were about to change. In 1846, the British Government appointed James Bruce (1811-63) Governor General of Canada, with orders to allow the majority party to rule the colony. Also known as Lord Elgin, he was the second son of Thomas Bruce, seventh Earl of Elgin, and eleventh Earl of Kincardine in Scotland. He arrived in Canada in 1847. In 1848 Elgin considered that the time was ripe to transfer decision-making powers to an elected parliament, and he recognized the legitimacy of this new responsible government — a cause for which the *Patriotes* had rebelled in 1837 and 1838.

The Liberal union government of Lafontaine-Baldwin introduced and passed the Rebellion Losses Bill in 1849, seeking to fairly compensate those who had suffered damages as a result of the acts of British troops crushing the *Patriote* Rebellion in 1837 and 1838.

A furor ensued! There were charges of betrayal and insult from the Lower Canadian Loyalists and the Château Clique, an elite Lower Canada group, connected by family, conservative ideology and commercial interests, that opposed reform and frequently clashed with elected officials. There were riots and demonstrations. The Tories pressured Lord Elgin, Governor General of Canada and the supreme authority in the land, to refuse royal assent. But times had changed: neither the Crown nor its representative was prepared to interfere with the legislation adopted by a duly elected assembly. Not everyone accepted Elgin's decision, however.

On April 25, 1849 Elgin drove into Montreal from Monklands, the Governor General's residence, and he gave royal assent to the bill. That night mobs set fire to the Parliament Building in Montreal.

The Burning of the Parliament Building in Montreal, 1849.
Oil on wood, attributed to Joseph Légaré (1795-1855).

Gift of Hugh Mackay, through W. D. Lighthall, McCord Museum, M11588

The Monklands estate was purchased in 1795 by James Monk, Chief Justice of Lower Canada. It was land that had previously been owned by the Décarie family. The first Monk residence was built there in 1804. Monklands was leased to the Crown when Parliament moved to Montreal in the early 1840s and it became a residence for the Governors of Canada. It was occupied by Sir Charles Metcalfe, Lord Cathcart and Lord Elgin. After the Parliament Building was burned in 1849 and Parliament left Montreal, the estate was briefly a country hotel.

In 1854 the sisters of the Congrégation de Notre-Dame purchased the estate and opened the Villa Maria boarding school. The Villa Maria still occupies the original residence, one of the oldest remaining Palladian-style villas in Canada. It was declared a historic monument in 1951.

James Bruce, Lord Elgin, circa 1855.
Oil on canvas by Cornelius Krieghoff (1815-72).
Gift of Arnold Wainwright, McCord Museum, M22464

"Monklands"
Former residence of the Governors and Governor General of Canada, Montreal, 1893. Photograph.

Gift of Stanley G. Triggs, McCord Museum, MP-0000.805.7

Peter McGill
Mayor of Montreal

Montreal was run by justices of the peace appointed by the Governor until Jacques Viger became the first elected mayor in 1833. Viger was a well-known *Patriote* and founding member of the Saint-Jean-Baptiste Society. One of his first initiatives was to provide the city with a coat of arms, which bears a cross remarkably similar to the St. Andrew's cross. In the four quarters are an English rose, an Irish shamrock, a Scottish thistle and a beaver to represent the French in Canada. By 1838 the beaver had become a Canadian symbol and on the Montreal coat of arms it was replaced by the *fleur de lys* (the stylized lily associated with the French monarchy) to represent Montreal's French roots.

Peter McGill was Montreal's second mayor. Born Peter McCutcheon in Scotland in 1789, he arrived in Montreal in 1809 and embarked on a career in the import-export trade. His uncle, John McGill (a resident of Toronto and no relation to James) promised to bequeath Peter his fortune if he adopted the McGill family name.

In 1821, with the merger of the North West and Hudson's Bay companies, Montreal lost its key role in the fur-trading network, supplanted by the posts on Hudson Bay. Peter McGill understood the need to diversify and shifted his investments out of fur into new staples (wheat, flour and lumber), transportation (shipping and railways), real estate and utilities. Like many other Scots in Montreal, McGill took advantage of the fact that the city was the main gateway to the North American interior. He moved into banking and finance. Peter McGill was Montreal's mayor in a period of considerable tension, from 1840 to 1842, shortly after the *Patriote* rebellions. He died in Montreal in 1860. The downtown Montreal municipal electoral district is named Peter McGill in his honour.

Peter McGill.
Photograph copied by William Notman and painted circa 1861.

Gift of the McGill University Library, McCord Museum, M15314

Gown owned by Mrs. A. W. Ogilvie, 1860.
Silk satin with evening bodice.

Gift of Mrs. Hugh Phillips, McCord Museum, M974.15.1-4

View of the Champ de Mars
MONTREAL.
Published by A. Bourne, Montreal, 1830.

View of the Champ de Mars, Montreal (with the St. Gabriel Street Church in the background.)
Robert Auchmuty Sproule (1799-1845.) Ink, watercolour on paper, 1830.

Gift of David Ross McCord. McCord Museum, M327

The St. Lawrence, at Montreal.

The St. Lawrence at Montreal.
William Henry Bartlett (1809-54). Ink, watercolour on paper, 1841

Gift of Dr. Francis McLennan, McCord Museum, M16634

William McGillivray and his second wife, 1805-06.
Oil on canvas by William Berczy (1744-1813).

McCord Museum, M18683

Detail, ceremonial chain
worn by the President of the St. Andrew's Society of Montreal.
Circa 1835, silver.

St. Andrew's Society of Montreal

Lady Elgin, née Mary Louisa Lambton, daughter of Lord Durham and wife of Lord Elgin,
Governor General of the Provinces of British North America, 1847-54.
Oil on canvas, attributed to Théophile Hamel (1817-70), 1846-48.

Gift from McGill University, McCord Museum, M994.35.3

Register of the acts of baptism, marriage and burial
of the Scotch Presbyterian Church, St. Gabriel Street, 1844.

Gift of Michel Lavallée, McCord Museum, M2002.127.1

View of McGill Campus 1908-1913. Watercolour by Percy Erskine Nobbs (1875-1964).

McCord Museum, M988X.122

Simon McTavish's (unfinished) house on Mount Royal. Watercolour, late 19th century.

Gift of Victor Buchanan, McCord Museum, M21263

Lord Strathcona driving the last spike, CPR, Craigellachie, B.C., 1885.
Original photograph by Alexander Ross, 1885, hand coloured lantern slide copy
distributed by the Canadian Pacific Railway Company circa 1910.

Gift of Mr. Stanley G. Triggs, McCord Museum, MP-0000.25.971

Export cigarettes poster.

The Stewart Museum at the Fort, Île Sainte-Hélène

Ogilvie Flour Mills poster. Chromolithograph by Rolph, Smith & Co.
McCord Museum, ME985.220

The Church of Scotland

The Presbyterian Church, founded by Calvin in the 16th century, rejects the episcopal form
of church government. Instead, the "elders" or "presbyters" (from the Greek word *presbytes*), elected by the
people in the congregation, are responsible for choosing their minister.

Presbyterians are Christians who are distinguished by their austere dogma and anti-clericalism,
their strict observance of the Sabbath and long church services with prayers, hymn singing and usually
improvised sermons. Another unique feature is that a Presbyterian church serves a membership rather than a
parish. If for any reason some of its members are not happy with their church
or its minister, they can start another one.

The first Protestant place of worship in Quebec was a chapel built in Berthier in 1785 but the first Protestant *church* was erected in 1792 on St. Gabriel Street in Montreal; it came to be known as the St. Gabriel Street Church. Ministers of the Church of Scotland exercised the right to register marriages, baptisms and burials from 1759 (and those of the St. Gabriel Street Church from its founding in 1792), but it was only in 1806 that the Legislative Assembly of Lower Canada officially granted them this right — over the objections of the Catholic and Anglican churches, which wanted to reserve the privilege for themselves. There were sixteen Presbyterian churches in Montreal in 1890, most of them serving the Scottish community.

Berthier-en-Haut, the First Protestant place of worship in Lower Canada, 1885.
Oil on canvas by Henry Richard S. Bunnett (1845-1910).

Gift of David Ross McCord, McCord Museum, M1168

James Somerville (born in Tollcross, Scotland, 1775, died 1837) was a teacher in Quebec City when he agreed in 1802 to become minister of the St. Gabriel Street Church at the end of the school year. In the meantime, Reverend Robert Forrest, who was visiting Montreal, preached in the church. When Somerville arrived in 1803 to take up his post, the followers of the two reverends clashed. This touchy situation, along with the fact that the Presbyterian community was growing rapidly, led to the creation of the Scotch Presbyterian Church on St. Peter Street, later renamed St. Andrew's Church, the second Presbyterian church in Montreal. In 1918, the congregations of St. Andrew's and St. Paul's churches amalgamated and worshipped in St. Paul's Church, on Dorchester Street (now René-Lévesque Blvd). In 1930, the building was sold to the Collège de Saint-Laurent, dismantled stone by stone and rebuilt in Ville Saint-Laurent, where today it houses the Musée des maîtres et artisans du Québec. The St. Andrew's and St. Paul's congregation moved to a new church on Sherbrooke Street and Redpath, where it still stands.

St. Gabriel Street Church communion token (recto and verso), 1864-87.
Gift of the Estate of Reverend Robert Campbell, McCord Museum, M7461.125

St. Gabriel Street Church, circa 1865. Photograph by Alexander Henderson (1831-1918).

Purchase from John L. Russell, McCord Museum, MP-0000.10.174

The Fur Trade
A Partnership: French Canadians, Scots and Aboriginal People

The fur trade was big business. Between 1764 and 1786 there were 10,258,350 furs,
including 2,556,236 beaver pelts, shipped from Canada to Great Britain. The Lachine Rapids
prevented ships from sailing further inland up the St. Lawrence, so Montreal became the gateway
to a vast fur trading network.

Under the French Régime, intrepid coureurs de bois travelled the backcountry,
trading a variety of goods with Aboriginal people for beaver and other pelts which eventually made
their way to the workshops of garment makers catering to high society in France.

This lucrative trade, interrupted by the war, began again in earnest after the Conquest (1759).
But the coureurs de bois, now called voyageurs, soon formed mutually profitable partnerships
and trading agreements with the Scots. The voyageurs knew the land and were formidable traders. The Scots
were shrewd merchants and traders and they were unafraid to brave the wilds in search of furs, but most
important of all, they had access to the vast markets in the British Empire.

The voyageurs and merchants travelled along the Canadian waterways,
portaging as they went, heading for the Aboriginal camps where they traded goods for furs.
Scottish explorers Simon Fraser (1776-1862) and Alexander MacKenzie (1764-1820) expanded this vast
trading ground west to the Pacific Ocean and north to the Beaufort Sea.

The prestigious Beaver Club was founded in Montreal in 1785. To belong to the Beaver Club one had to have completed one trading voyage and spent at least one winter at one of the posts in the *Pays d'en haut*, as western and northwestern Canada was called at the time. The founders were seven French Canadians and twelve Scots, all traders who had completed the initiation rite between 1751 and 1775. Members dined together every second Wednesday evening in winter, which they spent in town. At each meeting, they were required to wear their medals, hung around their necks on a light blue ribbon. The blue ribbon refers to the emblem of the *Most Noble Order of the Garter*, founded by Edward III in 1348. Legend has it that the Countess of Salisbury, the King's mistress, dropped her garter at a royal ball. The King rushed to pick it up and handed it back to her. His action drew much amused murmuring, to which the King replied "*Honi soit qui mal y pense*" (Evil be he that thinks evil of it) — a heartfelt cry that became the Order's motto — and the King vowed to make this light blue ribbon such a prestigious emblem that even the noblest members of court would wear it with pride.

James McGill's Beaver Club medal, circa 1785, gold.
The date 1766 inscribed on it refers to the perilous first canoe trip
made by the young James to a trading post.
Gift of David Ross McCord, McCord Museum, M1149

Hypolitte Desrivières' Beaver Club medal, circa 1785, gold.

Gift of David Ross McCord, McCord Museum, M2611

In 1780 a group of enterprising Scots in Montreal founded the North West Company, seeking to break the Hudson's Bay Company's longstanding monopoly on the fur trade. They hired mainly French-Canadian voyageurs, who travelled deep inland and across the continent to trade for furs, defying the Hudson's Bay Company monopoly and the Royal Charter granting it exclusive trading rights for the land that drained into Hudson Bay. The North West Company quickly captured two-thirds of the market. The Hudson's Bay Company was not amused. After years of conflict and the occasional outbreak of violence, the two companies finally merged in 1821.

The North West Company hiring contracts were nearly all signed with French Canadians or Métis, and they were printed only in French by the Company — with a space for the hired man to sign his X. On the other hand, bills of lading describing the load in each canoe were filled out by English clerks and were in English only.

Agreement between Augustin Roy and the North West Company, 1804.

Gift of John McIntyre, McCord Museum, M2737

James McGill

In 1707 the Union of the Scottish and English parliaments opened the markets in the English colonies to Scottish merchants. Glasgow metal workers and members of the hammermen's guild, the McGill family seized the opportunity to diversify and become traders.

James McGill was born in Glasgow, Scotland, in 1744 and died in Montreal in 1813. He was an English- and French-speaking graduate of the University of Glasgow. He emigrated first to the United States, then to British North America. In 1766 he left Montreal for Lake Superior, to acquire furs for a Quebec City merchant, and by the following year, he was trading on his own account. Ten years later, his marriage to Marie-Charlotte Guillimin, widow of Joseph-Amable Trottier dit Desrivières, brought him into the Desrivières family circle, with its extensive knowledge of the fur trading territories. This further boosted his success in business.

A number of Scottish merchants followed McGill's example and married French Canadian women, and such marriages were common at the time. The men's families benefited from the French Canadians' familiarity with the land, while their wives' families gained profitable ties with the new merchants. McGill was a highly influential figure in his day. In 1792, he was elected to represent the riding of Montreal West in the House of Assembly for Lower Canada, where his candidacy for the speakership was a tribute to his fluent French and English. In 1801, along with John Richardson, another Scot, and Jean-Marie Mondelet, he was charged with planning the demolition of the fortification walls — for Montreal was expanding quickly — and proposing a new city plan. He played major civil and political roles until his death.

James McGill belonged to the Montreal Militia, civilian volunteers who helped the army defend the city or maintain order. When American rebels drew near to Montreal in 1775, he was part of the group that negotiated the city's surrender, but his house was a Loyalist meeting place during the seven-month long American occupation. In 1787, McGill was made a major, much to his delight, and in 1810, he became the colonel commandant of the 1st Battalion of the Montreal Militia.

James McGill, who was considered the wealthiest Montrealer by his contemporaries, left property and large amounts of money to his widow, to the son he had with her, and to his wife's sons, whom he had adopted. But he also left a large number of donations to various charities in Montreal, Quebec City and Glasgow.

Portrait of James McGill, circa 1800-10.
Oil on canvas by Louis Dulongpré (1754-1843).

Gift of McGill University, McCord Museum, M970X.106

There was a stream on James McGill's property, and his house was called Burnside, meaning next to a stream. When McGill died suddenly in 1813, he left his house and estate, along with £10,000 (about $50,000 at the time) to the Royal Institution for the Advancement of Learning. He attached as condition to this enormous bequest that a college or university be founded on the grounds and that the college or one of the colleges of the university bear the name McGill.

Eight years later, McGill College (today McGill University) obtained its charter, but still existed only on paper. By 1823, the deadline for the bequest, the founders of the Montreal Medical Institution and the College authorities had agreed that the medical school would become McGill College's first faculty, thus fulfilling the conditions of the McGill bequest.

Burnside, 1875-1900.
Etching by John H. Macnaughton, after a sketch by William Busby Lambe (1826-98).

McCord Museum, M989X.66

Simon McTavish

"Fortune has proved so kind a Mistress to me for some past years."
— Simon McTavish, 1776

Simon McTavish was born in Strath, Scotland, in 1750; he died in Montreal in 1804. He came from an impoverished Scottish family. His father was a lieutenant in the 78th Fraser Highlanders, who took part in the siege of Louisbourg before returning to Scotland in 1763, when the regiment was disbanded.

In 1764, at age fourteen, the young and penniless Simon sailed for New York. He knew no one when he arrived but found a position as a clerk. From there, he advanced himself and began to climb the social ladder. By 1772, he was in Detroit, working in the fur trade. He then moved to Montreal where he joined other Scottish merchants who founded the North West Company, which he headed for a number of years. His nephews Duncan and William McGillivray joined him in Montreal. In 1793 he married Marie-Marguerite Chaboillez, daughter of an influential Montreal merchant. They had four children who, on their father's death, shared the largest fortune amassed by a Montreal businessman in the latter 18th century, some £125,000, or $625,000 at the time! After McTavish died in 1804, construction was halted on the new house he was building on the slopes of Mount Royal.

Intriguing stories were told about the unfinished mansion that stood abandoned for many years, frightening neighbourhood children with its ghostly air.

Simon McTavish.
Oil on canvas by Donald Richings Hill (1900-39).

Gift of David Ross McCord, McCord Museum, M1587

Many Scotsmen spent the winter in the trading posts, and these long stays created opportunities for exchanges of all kinds. Some of them took country wives — a polite name for Native mistresses. They thus contributed to a blending of cultures, as well as of blood or "races," as was said at the time.

Marriages "in the custom of the country" usually served the interests of both the Aboriginal community and the trading company. These unions were encouraged by the Native communities, as they gave them an entry into their trading partners' families, along with increased protection and patronage helping ensure a steady supply of trade goods. The wives would help the traders run the trading post and prepare for their fur-trading voyages. As for the husband and wife, they found support, protection and quite often love. Such mixed marriages became so common that a new mixed-blood group gradually appeared — the Métis. With a foot in both cultures, these individuals were long sought after by fur traders as voyageurs, interpreters, guides and clerks.

Letitia, a Métis woman from Manitoba, 1858.
Photograph by Humphrey Lloyd Hime.

McCord Museum, MP-0000.1453.28

William McGillivray

William McGillivray was born in Dunlichty, Scotland, in 1764 and died in 1825. His uncle, Simon McTavish, paid for his studies and those of his brothers Simon and Duncan. McTavish brought William to Montreal in 1784, and he worked as a clerk in various North West Company trading posts. Around 1790 at Fort William (today Thunder Bay), William McGillivray took as a country wife a Métis woman named Susan. They had four children. Ten years later, he married Magdalen McDonald, sister of another leading fur merchant. She bore him six children.

In 1790, McGillivray became a company partner and, on McTavish's death in 1804, his successor as head of the company. All his brothers and the children from his first marriage worked in the fur trade for the North West Company.

When he died, in 1825, McGillivray left his estate in Scotland and £10,000 to each of his two daughters from his second marriage. To his two sons Simon and Joseph, the only surviving children of his first marriage, he left £2,000 each and his lands in Plantagenet Township, in the Ottawa Valley.

William McGillivray (1764-1825).
Oil on canvas by unknown artist, before 1784.

McCord Museum, M18682.

Education and the Professions

Presbyterianism, which in 1690 became the state religion in Scotland, encourages everyone to read the Scriptures for themselves. As a result, from these early days, in Scotland rich and poor alike learned to read and to value individual and collective knowledge. In 1776 Adam Smith wrote in his *Wealth of Nations* that "[in Scotland,] almost the whole common people [know how] to read, and a very great proportion of them to write and account." The Scots who settled in Montreal were generally better educated than their fellow citizens. With their acute awareness of the importance of a good education, they quickly took the lead in developing English-language institutions. One of the keys to their success in Canada was education.

Alexander Skakel

Alexander Skakel (1776-1846) was born in Scotland. After graduation from King's College of Aberdeen, he came to Montreal in 1799, and shortly afterward opened the Classical and Mathematical School. It was a great success. In 1818, he was appointed Master of the Grammar School of Montreal, where pupils studied English, writing, arithmetic and accounting and, in the upper years, Latin, Greek, philosophy and science (or "natural philosophy," as it was known at the time). Skakel was a very active member of the community. He was a founding member of the Montreal Curling Club in 1807 (now the Royal Montreal Curling Club). He was a member of the Natural History Society of Montreal and, in 1820, he became a member of the management committee struck to found the Montreal General Hospital. He was reportedly also the one who recommended to James McGill that he bequeath his Burnside estate to create a university.

A number of other Scottish educators opened schools as soon as they arrived in Montreal. Ann Cuthbert Rae founded a boarding school for young girls on St. Vincent Street in 1815, and Reverend Edward Black opened an academy for boys near the St. Gabriel Street Church shortly after he came to Montreal in 1830.

In 1843, a group of merchants looking for a more "modern" education than that offered by the Grammar School of Montreal founded the High School of Montreal, patterned on one in Edinburgh. The two schools merged after Skakel's death in 1846.

Alexander Skakel.
Original painting photographically copied onto canvas by William Notman (1826-91),
painted in oil by Edward Sharpe in 1870.

Gift of the Montreal General Hospital, McCord Museum, N-0000.2.4

William Dawson
(later Sir William Dawson)

William Dawson (1820-99) was born of Scottish ancestry in Pictou, Nova Scotia, son of a bookseller, stationer and printer. He showed an insatiable curiosity from a very young age. He collected minerals, shells, fossils and specimens of all kinds, while acquiring a solid grounding in Latin, Greek and Hebrew. He studied geology and taxidermy at the University of Edinburgh in 1840, and returned there in 1847 to study chemistry — and to marry Margaret Ann Young Mercer, whom he had met during his first stay. Before he joined McGill, Dawson took part in many exploratory field trips, particularly in Nova Scotia and Upper and Lower Canada, seeking coal, iron, copper and phosphate deposits.

He was just 35 in 1855 when he was offered the position of principal of McGill College, which would become McGill University in 1885. He turned it into a modern, world-renowned university that included a teacher's college, scientific chairs in botany, meteorology and applied mineralogy and a faculty of engineering. In addition to his administrative responsibilities, he continued to teach chemistry, agriculture, geology, zoology and botany and to continue his research in geology and paleontology. He even found time to create parks. Dawson's achievements were many and varied, but McGill was his major achievement. Humorist Stephen Leacock, an economics professor at McGill, would quite justly say of him that "More than that of any one or group of men, McGill is *his* work."

In the late 19th century, William Dawson was the first to study the plant fossils from the Miguasha cliffs in the Gaspé Peninsula; this region has now been recognized as a UNESCO World Heritage Site representing the Devonian period.

On the basis of his research, Dawson was inclined to admit that the Earth might date back millions of years, although this conflicted with his strongly held creationist beliefs. However, he refused to acknowledge Darwin's theory of evolution.

In 1860, when excavations at the corner of Metcalfe and Burnside (today de Maisonneuve Boulevard) turned up a number of Aboriginal objects, Dawson launched Canada's first archaeological salvage operation. Large quantities of potsherds and bone and stone artifacts, all predating the arrival of Europeans, were discovered, and for a long time it was believed that this site was part of Hochelaga, the Iroquoian village described by Jacques Cartier in 1535. More recent analyses of the "Dawson site" tend to show, however, that it was an even older village, possibly dating to the 15th century.

Sir William Dawson was a remarkable scientist and educator who maintained his insatiable intellectual curiosity until his death in Montreal in 1899.

Sir William Dawson, 1891-92.
Oil on canvas by Wyatt Eaton (1849-96).

Visual Arts Collection, McGill University, 73-270

William Logan
(later Sir William Logan)

William Logan (1798-1875) was born in Montreal to Scottish parents. He began his secondary studies at Alexander Skakel's Grammar School and completed them in Edinburgh, where he enrolled in the faculty of medicine. A chemistry professor there introduced him to neptunism, a new theory claiming that all stratified rocks had been formed underwater. Logan went on to work for twenty years for an uncle who owned mines and quarries, prospecting for coal for him. Logan returned to Canada in 1842 as the first Director of the Geological Survey of Canada, charged with the task of drawing a geological map of Canada, and to make sure that the Survey found coal deposits. In good Scots tradition, science, along with education and industry, would be handmaiden to social progress.

William Logan's work was so visionary and painstakingly accurate that the Geological Survey of Canada continues to rely on it even today.

Sir William Logan was knighted by Queen Victoria in 1856. He died in Wales in 1875. Canada's highest peak, Mount Logan (5,959 metres) is named after this outstanding scientist.

Sir William Edmond Logan, geologist, Montreal, 1865.
Photograph by William Notman (1826-91).

Purchase from Associated Screen News Ltd., McCord Museum, I-16533.1

Percy Erskine Nobbs

Percy Erskine Nobbs (1875-1964) was born and educated in Scotland. He was a pupil of Robert Lorimer, a Scottish architect who was a leading figure in the Arts and Crafts movement. In 1903 Nobbs was appointed to the Macdonald Chair of Architecture, and named Director of the School of Architecture (1903-13) at McGill University. In addition to his academic duties he remained in active practice as an architect, but always in partnership with a practicing architect. He designed many buildings on the McGill campus as well as commercial and residential buildings. His work includes the main Birks Building (1911) at Ste-Catherine and Phillips Square, and the Drummond Medical Building (constructed in 1930 and still standing on Drummond north of Ste-Catherine Street) with its distinctive outdoor iron canopy.

When Nobbs gave up his position as Director of the School of Architecture he continued to combine his practice with teaching until his retirement in 1940. With associates Hutchison and Wood he designed the McGill University Student Union Building (1906), which now houses the McCord Museum. Nobbs and his partner George Taylor Hyde designed many beautiful Arts and Crafts-inspired residences in Montreal and the surrounding area and the graceful and harmonious University Club of Montreal, still considered by many to be an architectural masterwork.

Prof. Percy Erskine Nobbs, architect, 1906.
Photograph by William Notman & Son.

Purchase from Associated Screen News Ltd., McCord Museum, II-159967

William Macdonald

William Macdonald was the founder of the Macdonald Tobacco Company and a great benefactor to McGill University, and to the Montreal General Hospital. Macdonald wanted a college to provide practical instruction for young people who would go out to work in rural English-speaking communities in Quebec and eastern Canada, so he underwrote the construction of Macdonald College (part of McGill University) and gave it a $2 million endowment. When it opened in 1907, the college had 115 teachers-in-training, 62 students in household science and 38 in agriculture, as well as a teaching staff of 37 and a principal.

Macdonald College, Sainte-Anne-de-Bellevue, 1920.
Photograph by William Notman & Son.
Purchase from Associated Screen News Ltd., McCord Museum, VIEW-19540

Household Science class, Macdonald College, Sainte-Anne de-Bellevue, 1909.
Photograph by William Notman & Son.

Purchase from Associated Screen News Ltd., McCord Museum, II-175978.

The Donaldas

Very few women are included in 19th-century history. At that time, as soon as a woman married, her civil status was reduced to that of a child. With no right to vote and no independent legal existence, a married woman was expected to pursue one or both of two options: homemaking and childrearing, and charitable work. If there was enough money to support the family, working outside the home was frowned upon. Unmarried women who needed to work outside the home were very restricted in their choice of employment, especially young women whose families were anxious to preserve their social standing in the eyes of their peers. These women were expected to select only a "respectable" profession such as nursing or teaching young children and girls. There was little or no question of women pursuing higher education. In 1884 Helen Reid passed the entrance examinations to McGill University—and was refused admission. The principal claimed that the university lacked the necessary funds to handle women students. Helen promptly appealed to Scots fur trader and railway magnate Donald Smith (later Lord Strathcona) who immediately signed a cheque for $50,000 to the university, stipulating that the money was to be used only for higher education for women. The first women admitted were affectionately called the Donaldas, in tribute to Smith. He continued to support them, providing most of the funds to build Royal Victoria College, which was a residence, a teaching institution and an intellectual centre for women at McGill. Helen Reid established the McGill University School of Social Work. As Reid herself put it: "Women maintained their charity and their grace, but ... threw off the yoke of convention and took their place alongside their brothers." (1892)

Donalda Group, 1898.
Photograph by William Notman & Son.

Purchase from Associated Screen News Ltd., McCord Museum, II-123244

In the early 18th century there was a great increase in immigration to Canada. Many of the immigrants were poor and in ill health, particularly after long and difficult sea voyages. Healthcare needs were overwhelming.

The Female Benevolent Society and the Society for the Relief of Immigrants and other charitable groups were formed to do good works for the needy. Soup kitchens were installed and schools were set up for the children where they were taught "domestic work, reading and writing and the fear of God." But more care of the sick was needed, and the charitable groups campaigned for a large modern hospital to meet the needs of a growing population. In 1818 a small hospital of four beds was opened. In 1819 a 24-bed facility opened on Craig Street, the Montreal General Hospital. A new building was soon built on Dorchester (now René-Lévesque) just east of St-Laurent Boulevard. This building is now the St-Charles-Boromée chronic care facility. In 1955 the Montreal General moved to its present site on the edge of Mount Royal.

In 1822, the team of doctors at the newly founded Montreal General Hospital began lobbying its directors to create a school of medicine along the lines of the one at the University of Edinburgh, where they had all studied. After all, they reasoned, the Scottish institution was famous worldwide for its "clinical teaching" approach. The Montreal Medical Institution opened its doors the following year, admitting 25 students. Although McGill College existed only on paper at the time, an agreement was struck with McGill authorities, making the Institution its first faculty. As James McGill had stipulated in his will, an institution of higher learning was founded in Montreal within ten years of his death.

Montreal General Hospital, circa 1875.
Photograph by James George Parks.

McCord Museum, MP-0000.3141

William Robertson

William Robertson (1784-1844) entered the Faculty of Medicine at the University of Edinburgh in 1802. In 1805, while sailing to Canada to report for his position as a British army medical orderly, he was shipwrecked off Cape Breton. He barely escaped drowning, and found shelter in the home of the Attorney General, William Campbell. There he met Campbell's daughter—his future wife, with whom he went on to have twelve children. Robertson arrived in Montreal in 1815, and by 1818 was part of the medical team at the small institution that would become the Montreal General Hospital in 1822. He was the first to conduct an operation there, when he amputated a patient's leg. He later became a founding member and director of the Montreal Medical Institution, where he would teach obstetrics and women's and children's health. He was one of the remarkable foursome of Edinburgh-trained doctors who initially directed the Montreal General Hospital. He died in Montreal in 1844.

Robertson was also a justice of the peace, in charge of maintaining order during elections. In 1832, when close election results in Montreal West brought people out into the streets, he read the Riot Act to the crowd. The British soldiers then fired on the demonstrators, killing three. When Louis-Joseph Papineau accused Robertson of giving the order to fire, Robertson challenged him to a duel. Papineau refused, stating that his comments were directed not at the man personally, but at him in his capacity as magistrate.

Dr. William Robertson.
Oil on canvas by Robert Harris (1849-1919).

Visual Arts Collection, McGill University, 75-013

Merchants and Industrialists

Montreal in the 19th century was a bustling city of billowing smokestacks,
clattering carriages, noisy factories and the bells and whistles of ships in a busy harbour.

Leading the way in this booming drive for industrialization was a new generation
of Scottish immigrants who chose to settle in Montreal, Canada's metropolis at the time
and a major continental hub. Bolstered by their solid education, well-honed business sense, valuable contacts
in the worlds of finance and politics and, above all, a will to succeed that was actually encouraged, rather
than discouraged, by their religion, these men of often modest origins
would go on to build empires and fortunes. Under their guidance, vast red brick
factories sprang up like mushrooms along the Lachine Canal
and near the harbour.

The Allans

Hugh Allan (1810-82), later Sir Hugh Allan, was born in Scotland. He emigrated to Montreal in 1826. He rose quickly from a clerk position in a merchandising company. Within ten years he bought ships to extend the shipping part of the business, using the latest technology for his Montreal Ocean Steamship Co. It would become Canada's leading shipping company. He moved into railroads and in 1872 organized a syndicate that became the Canadian Pacific Railway Co. (CPR). His political contributions to the Conservative Party and the CPR contract to build the railway to British Columbia fuelled the Pacific Scandal. Allan very successfully diversified into coal mines, factories, banking and insurance. Although he supported the Montreal Sailor's Institute, he was not known for his charitable contributions. He was knighted by Queen Victoria in 1871.

Hugh Andrew Allan (1860-1951), later Sir Hugh Montagu Allan, was the second son of Sir Hugh Allan. When he was twenty-one years old he began working for the Allan Line, at the time owned by his father and his uncle Andrew. He changed his name to Hugh Montagu Allan to avoid confusion with his cousin Hugh Andrew Allan. Thereafter he was known as Montagu Allan. He directed the company for a number of years, and also headed the Merchant's Bank before it merged with the Bank of Montreal in 1929.

The Merchant's Bank head office was built for Hugh Allan, Senior in 1870 on the corner of Saint-Jacques and Saint-Pierre streets in Old Montreal, and it was enlarged in 1899 by his son Montagu Allan. Some parts of the magnificent interior of this building have been restored and the building re-opened in 2002 as a boutique hotel.

Sir Montagu Allan was knighted in 1904 and was an honorary Lieutenant-Colonel in the Black Watch. He was an avid sportsman, longtime president of the Montreal Jockey Club, and a member of many other clubs. In 1910 he donated the Allan Cup for competition in amateur hockey. Sadly, he and his wife Marguerite Ethel Mackenzie (1873-1947) lost their son in the First World War, and two of their daughters drowned when the *Lusitania* sank in 1915; their only surviving child, Marguerite, predeceased them in 1942.

(*Above*) Sir Hugh Montagu Allan, Honorary Lieutenant-Colonel in the Black Watch, 1913. Photograph by William Notman & Son.

Purchase from Associated Screen News Ltd., McCord Museum, II-195950

(*Right*) Allan Line. Summer Service, 1871. Engraving by John Henry Walker, printed by A. A. Stevenson.

McCord Museum, M989X.69

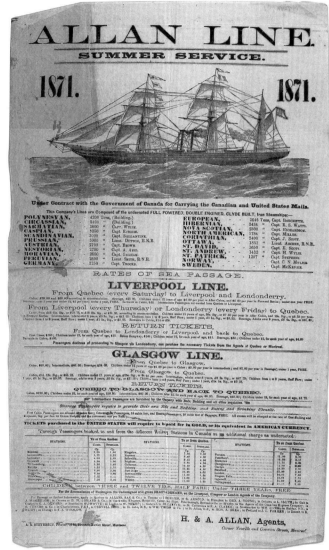

In 1860 Sir Hugh Allan bought the McTavish estate on Mount Royal and built the extravagant residence, Ravenscrag. The house was an Italian Renaissance-style showpiece. It had 34 rooms, including a conservatory, a library, a billiard room and a large ballroom. Each room featured a different architectural style. The house included a tower with an excellent view of the Port of Montreal, the St. Lawrence River and much of the city of Montreal.

When Sir Hugh Allan died in 1882 the house was taken over by his son Montagu Allan. Sir Montagu Allan donated Ravenscrag to the Royal Victoria Hospital in honour of his father in the 1940s, and it was renamed the Allan Memorial Institute in 1943. There have been many alterations to the interior of the building to accommodate the Allan Memorial Institute, a psychiatric facility that is part of the McGill University Health Centre.

Sir Hugh Montagu Allan's house, Ravenscrag, Pine Avenue, Montreal, 1902.
Photograph by William Notman & Son.

Purchase from Associated Screen News Ltd., McCord Museum II-143394

William Christopher McDonald
(later Sir William Christopher Macdonald)

In the mid-18th century, after the Jacobites suffered their final defeat, Scottish Catholics found themselves under great pressure to convert to Protestantism. Captain John MacDonald preferred to lead a group of Catholic followers into exile rather than yield. In 1771 he purchased 20,000 acres of farmland in the Tracadie region on Prince Edward Island, from a man named James Montgomery. He brought 210 Highlanders there in 1772. A veritable microcosm of Scottish society of the time, these MacDonalds, MacEacherns, MacKenzies, MacPhees, Beatons, Campbells, Gillises, MacRaes, MacIntoshes, MacKinnons and others founded the settlement of Glenaladale. John's grandsons, brothers Augustine and William Christopher Macdonald (1831-1917) [Macdonald spelled his name McDonald until 1898] arrived in Montreal in 1852, and built their first tobacco factory in 1858, importing the raw material from Kentucky. In 1866, William became the sole owner, and the company was renamed W. C. McDonald Tobacco. By 1871, over 500 employees were busy producing chewing and pipe tobacco.

In the 1870s the plant moved to east-end Hochelaga. This plant employed some 1,100 workers at that time, just over half of them women. Although Macdonald abhorred the use of his own products, tobacco gave him the funds he needed for his philanthropic work—the only thing that truly mattered to this reclusive bachelor. Most of Macdonald's largesse went to one educational institution, McGill University, nearly always to found scientific and technical colleges and faculties.

Macdonald had no children so he left his company to the two sons of his assistant, David Stewart, and he donated $1 million to Macdonald College, $500,000 to the McGill Faculty of Medicine, $300,000 to the McGill Conservatory of Music and $500,000 to the Montreal General Hospital. David MacDonald Stewart (1920-84) later inherited Macdonald Tobacco and sold it in 1973. He invested the proceeds from the sale into the Macdonald Stewart Foundation, a philanthropic institution that continues to support many initiatives in education, medicine, heritage conservation and culture, including the Stewart Musem at the Fort, Île Sainte-Hélène.

Sir William Christopher Macdonald.
Oil on canvas (posthumous portrait 1917-18) by Robert Harris (1849-1919).

Gift of Mrs. Walter S. Stewart, McCord Museum, M970.65

The Macdonald Tobacco Company used images of Highlanders to promote its products. Macdonald was not the first, or the last, to use images of proud Scotland to sell tobacco products. While some tobacconists stood a wooden Indian outside their shops, others used images of a Highland warrior or a ravishing young woman to attract customers. The custom may have come from the 18th century, when the Tobacco Lords of Glasgow made a fortune by controlling trade in tobacco imported from North America.

Highland Lassie, McNee & Sons, London, Ontario.
Colour lithography by Rolph and Clark, 1904-17.

Gift of BCE Inc., McCord Museum, M999.70.6.20

Macdonald Tobacco factory, 1880. Photograph.

The Stewart Museum at the Fort, Île Sainte-Hélène

The Ogilvies

Alexander Walker Ogilvie (1829-1902) was the eldest son of eleven children. He was born on his father's farm in Côte–St.Michel (the area that is now St-Léonard) near Montreal. His father (Alexander Ogilvie, Sr.) also operated a flour mill, probably in the Des Récollets faubourg, in partnership with his brother-in-law William Watson. Another uncle of Alexander Walker Ogilvie, James Goudie, was also a miller and one of his father's partners. It was with Goudie that Alexander junior joined forces in 1852 to operate his first flour mill. In 1855 Goudie left the business and Alexander Walker founded A.W. Ogilvie & Co., millers and grain merchants, working in partnership with his younger brother John; younger brother William Watson Ogilvie (1835-1900) joined them in 1860.

No one could accuse Alexander Ogilvie of having limited horizons. Along with his business and financial activities (he was one of the first shareholders of the Sun Life Assurance Co.), he was an enthusiastic politician, he was active in charitable organizations and he served as a director of the Mount Royal Cemetery. He withdrew from the administration of the mill in 1874. As a bilingual member of the Liberal-Conservative Party and an ardent advocate of Canadian Confederation, he acted as the liaison between the French-speaking and English-speaking deputations. He was appointed a senator in 1881.

Excerpts from the Diary of A.W. Ogilvie, 1851, 1852

May 7 – I am twenty two years of age today. I was sowing grass seed all day, in the evening I visit to Hastings with the onion sower. *June 5* – William brought out a coloured man to hire (as Louis' time was nigh up) he is a runaway slave and only about a fortnight free. The weather still very wet. *July 1* – In the afternoon, Janet McGibbon, Fanny and I went down to Mr. Leney's, we had tea there and Sarah [Sarah Leney, his future spouse] came as far as Mrs. Muirhead's. *July 4* – Sunday […] There was an appearance of a shower. J.S. and Jenny and Sarah and I waited till about 8 o'clock, but we had to come away in the rain. I spent a few happy hours in the barn. Coming down the alley it was so muddy, Sarah lost her shoe and I carried them down to the house. *September 21* – Lord Elgin came into town this morning about 2 o'clock for the first time since he was hooted out of the city. He met with a very cool reception.

A.W. Ogilvie's farm house, Côte St. Michel, near Montreal, 1866.
Photograph by William Notman (1826-91).

Purchase from Associated Screen News Ltd., McCord Museum, I-21173

This silk satin tartan gown inspired by the Ogilvie tartan was owned by Sarah Leney Ogilvie (née Sarah Leney). It would have been worn at formal gatherings and might have been worn by Sarah at the ball given in honour of the Prince of Wales, who had come to inaugurate the Victoria Bridge in 1860. Sarah's husband, Alexander Walker Ogilvie, was one of the organizers of the reception, and Mrs. Ogilvie herself most likely took a turn tripping the light fantastic with the Prince that evening. His Royal Highness with his entourage arrived at the ball about ten p.m. and remained until four in the morning, having danced twenty of the twenty-one dances.

The gown dates from a period of renewed pride in Scottish heritage, when traditional Highland symbols such as tartans were being elevated to high fashion by trendsetters like Queen Victoria, coinciding with her acquisition of Balmoral Castle in 1852. The dress consists of a skirt and two separate bodices, one that was a low-necked, short-sleeved bodice intended for a formal evening occasion such as a ball, and a second made to be worn with a long-sleeved and high-necked lace underbodice and intended for afternoon receptions. In an era where the cost of fabric could far exceed that of the making up of a dress, two bodices were frequently made to enable a woman to get the most mileage out of her fabric investment in the voluminous skirt.

Gown owned by Mrs. A. W. Ogilvie, 1860.
Silk satin with evening bodice.

Gift of Mrs. Hugh Phillips, McCord Museum, M974.15.1-4

The history of the Ogilvie family empire is dominated by three brothers: Alexander Walker, who managed its financial affairs; John, in charge of obtaining supplies of wheat and expanding into Upper Canada; and William Watson, who saw to administration in Montreal. Following their father's example and creating a network of professional and family ties, they built the largest flour milling concern in the country, with elevators and mills reaching as far west as settlers and the railway could take them.

William Watson Ogilvie ruled the mill with an iron fist. He was a shrewd businessman and a prominent member of the Montreal business elite. He was president of the Montreal Board of Trade (1893-94), and a director of the Bank of Montreal. He was also a generous philanthropist.

Aside from his work, William W. Ogilvie had two other great passions: horses and travel. In 1892, William Watson Ogilvie purchased a huge farm dating from the 17th century, near the Lachine rapids. There he had a new house built, where he spent summers with his family. He had a stable for his Ayrshire cattle and another for his expensive racehorses, which he also rode while hunting on his lands. He died in 1900, followed in 1902 by his brother Alexander Walker Ogilvie. The mills were subsequently sold to a Canadian syndicate which included Sir Montagu Allan and Sir George Alexander Drummond.

William Watson Ogilvie, 1888.
Photograph by William Notman & Son.

Purchase from Associated Screen News Ltd., McCord Museum, II-87527

The Redpaths

John Redpath was born in Earlston, Scotland, in 1796; he died in Montreal in 1869. Redpath was a stone mason's apprentice who became a sugar king. He was only 20 years old when he arrived in Canada from Scotland in 1816. Yet within just a few years, this stone mason's name was on everyone's lips in Montreal's financial and industrial circles. Redpath was an astute entrepreneur who tapped into the enormous demand for masons at the time to become an important building contractor. In partnership with Thomas McKay, Andrew White and Thomas Phillips, John Redpath contracted to build part of the Lachine Canal (1825). In partnership with Robert Drummond he built part of the Rideau Canal (1827-28) between Bytown (now Ottawa) and Kingston. He also worked on the Montreal General Hospital, the new Notre-Dame Church and some of the first McGill University buildings.

Redpath was elected to the board of directors of the Bank of Montreal in 1833, and remained a director for the rest of his life. He made investments in Montreal's booming economy and in the rest of Canada, in banks, insurance and mines. In 1854, with the fortune he had amassed, he began building Canada's first sugar refinery along the Lachine Canal. The silhouette of the seven-storey Redpath smokestacks would stand out against the Montreal skyline for many years after their owner came up with the brilliant idea of refining raw sugar in Canada. His industrial complex, erected in 1854, was so impressive that Montrealers came to visit the worksite on Sundays. Redpath was one of the first to set up shop near the Saint-Gabriel lock on the Lachine Canal. This area would soon become Canada's leading industrial park. One year after it opened, the refinery, later known as the Canada Sugar Refinery Company Ltd., had 100 employees, refining cane sugar brought from the West Indies on the *Helen Drummond* and the *Grace Redpath*, company ships named after John Redpath's daughter and daughter-in-law. (His daughter Helen married George Drummond and Grace was the wife of his son Peter.)

John Redpath was an important benefactor for the Montreal General Hospital and the Mechanic's Institute (now the Atwater Library) and many other charitable organizations.

John Redpath, 1836.
Oil on canvas by Antoine Plamondon (1804-95).

Gift of McGill University, McCord Museum, M994.35.1

John Redpath was twice a husband, seventeen times a father, always a Presbyterian. As a devout Presbyterian and a member of the council of elders at St. Paul's Church, he oversaw the Sunday school until the church split in 1845. He then became a founding member of the Free Church on Côté Street. His family life was just as busy. Janet McPhee, with whom he shared his first years in Canada after they married in 1818, bore him ten children. He had seven more children with Jane Drummond, whom he wed shortly after being widowed in 1834. He maintained longstanding business and social links with the Drummond family in Edinburgh. Jane was born in 1815, just three years before John left for Canada. In 1854, Redpath brought over Jane's younger brother, George Alexander Drummond, to put him in charge of technical operations at Redpath Sugar. In 1857, Drummond married Redpath's daughter Helen, combining romance and business as a recipe for success.

Jane Drummond, second wife of John Redpath, 1836.
Oil on canvas by Antoine Plamondon (1804-95).

Gift of McGill University, McCord Museum, M994.35.2

Of John Redpath's seventeen children, only Peter Redpath (1821-94) would be involved in the Redpath Sugar business from its start in 1854. Today, however, Peter Redpath is known mainly as a philanthropist. He underwrote one of Canada's first museums, the Redpath Museum. The Redpath opened its doors in 1882. Some of the main displays were Sir William Dawson's paleontological collections. In 19th-century Montreal, trade and industry created the individual wealth that enriched society as a whole, through philanthropic endeavours in many fields, including education. Trade and industry in turn drew on various aspects of the research and scientific advances that education made possible. While John Redpath made generous contributions to religious and social charities, Peter Redpath supported education. McGill University was the main beneficiary.

Peter Redpath, 1892. Photograph by William Notman & Son.
Purchase from Associated Screen News Ltd., McCord Museum, II-99021

John Redpath's house "Terrace Bank", on Mountain north of Sherbrooke Street, Montreal, circa 1880.
Photograph copied by William Notman & Son in 1947.

Gift of George Dudkoff, McCord Museum, II-338494.0.1.

Montreal society had something of the quality of a tightly woven Scottish fabric. McGill University, founded by Scots, expanded thanks to generous donations from members of Montreal's Scottish community. The university often commissioned Scottish architects to design its buildings. One of these was Sir Andrew Taylor (born in Edinburgh, Scotland, in 1850; died in England in 1937) who arrived in Canada in 1883. He designed the Peter Redpath Library and other buildings. Sir Andrew was related through his mother to the Drummonds and Redpaths, and through his wife to Sir William Dawson, principal of the university at the time. The Redpath Museum was commissioned by Peter Redpath to house the collections of McGill Principal William Dawson. Today people would be up in arms over such conflict of interest, but at that time such alliances were common.

Interior, Redpath Museum, McGill University, 1925.
Photograph by Sydney Jack Hayward.

McCord Museum, MP-1980.83

Redpath Museum, McGill University, 1883.
Photograph by Alexander Henderson (1831-1913).

McCord Museum, MP-1982.26.

Peter Redpath Library, McGill University, circa 1893. Photograph by William Notman & Son.

Purchase from Associated Screen News Ltd., McCord Museum, VIEW-2674.A

The Railway Men

Canada's first transcontinental passenger train departed Montreal on June 28, 1886,
and arrived at the Port Moody station in British Columbia on July 4. To link Canadians from one ocean
to the other, two great railways had to be built and thousands of kilometres of track had to be laid.
All of this colossal enterprise was headed by Montreal Scots.

Donald Alexander Smith
(later Lord Strathcona)

Donald Alexander Smith, (born in Forres, Scotland in 1820, died in London in 1914), is better known as Lord Strathcona.

Smith's uncle John Stuart retired to his native Scotland after travelling through forests and down rivers with Scottish explorer Simon Fraser on behalf of the North West Company. Young Donald Smith was taken with his uncle's tales of adventure and he took passage for Lower Canada in 1838 with letters of recommendation in his pocket.

For a number of years he was a clerk for the Hudson's Bay Company. While Smith was managing the post at Rigolet, Labrador, he met Isabella Sophia, daughter of a man named Richard Hardisty, who had married "in the fashion of the country" the daughter of another Scottish clerk and a Native woman. Isabella had been the companion of James Grant since 1851, but the two separated after a son was born. Neither her unofficial marriage nor her divorce was legally valid in the eyes of God-fearing people. Smith actually solemnized their union three times — once in 1853, again in 1859 and a third time in 1896, in New York, witnessed by his Wall Street lawyers — but the couple never escaped the hint of scandal. Their devotion endured nonetheless. When Smith was travelling, he wrote or cabled his beloved Isabella every day. Smith rose to high position and influence in the Hudson's Bay Company, greatly expanding their land interests in the Northwest. He invested in railways for himself and the company and he was a director, vice-president, then president, of the Bank of Montreal. He invested in financial institutions, had interests in newspapers and entered the political arena. He became a prominent figure in Canadian business circles and an important social figure as well. His first peerage in 1896 was superseded by a second in 1900.

Smith became friends with Hugh and Andrew Allan, Richard Bladworth Angus and many others who would join him in the grand adventure of the Canadian Pacific Railway. He was a generous benefactor to many causes and institutions, notably McGill University, the Royal Victoria Hospital in Montreal, many other universities all over the world, the YMCA, churches, schools, clubs and the Boy Scouts.

Donald Alexander Smith, 1st Baron Strathcona and Mount Royal, 1895.
Photograph by William Notman & Son.

Purchase from Associated Screen News Ltd., McCord Museum, II-110266

George Stephen
(later Lord Mount Stephen)

George Stephen (1829-1921), the son of a woodworker, is better known as Lord Mount Stephen. He arrived in Montreal in 1850 and founded a woollen goods business with his cousin William. In 1873, with another cousin, Donald Smith (later Lord Strathcona), he tested the waters in the railway industry, building a part of the St. Paul–Winnipeg line. His great friend John A. Macdonald urged him to form a financial consortium with a view to building a transcontinental rail line to British Columbia. He let himself be convinced, and the rest is history.

George Stephen was the first Canadian to be knighted, in 1891, and he was dubbed Lord Mount Stephen. He was an extremely rich man, and a generous one. With his cousin Donald Smith he gave $1.8 million for the construction and operation of the Royal Victoria Hospital. He was also a great fishing enthusiast, with a huge estate at Grand-Métis, which he left to his niece Elsie Meighen Reford. The magnificent gardens she created there, now known as the Reford Gardens, are open to the public during the summer, a lasting legacy of the Scots of Montreal.

Lord Mount Stephen's elegant residence at 1440 Drummond Street in Montreal, now the Mount Stephen Club, was recently opened to the public for dining.

Bust of George Stephen, Lord Mount Stephen, 1886.
Carved marble, signed C. L. Gleichen (1835-91).

Gift of L. Alexis Reford, Boris Reford and Sonja Arnold-Forster,
McCord Museum, M986.275.1

Richard Angus

In 1857, a lowly bank employee named Richard Angus (born in Bathgate, Scotland, in 1831; died in Senneville, Quebec, in 1922) arrived in Montreal and immediately began working for the Bank of Montreal.

In 1861, when he was transferred to manage a branch in Chicago, he observed the flood of settlers heading toward the American West and realized that Canada had to prepare the way for its own settlers. The best solution was a transcontinental railway, to carry people and goods and assert Canada's sovereignty over its own territory. He returned to Montreal, and quickly rose to prominence and power within the bank, eventually becoming President. Angus invested personally in many ventures, and joined with three other Scots — Duncan McIntyre, Donald Smith and George Stephen — to found the Canadian Pacific Railway Company.

Montreal's Angus Shops were named for Richard Bladworth Angus. The Angus Shops opened in 1904 with the colossal mandate of producing and maintaining all Canadian Pacific rolling stock for Eastern Canada. The huge open-plan spaces made it possible to introduce assembly-line production, a first in Canada. The construction of the country's largest industrial complex also brought improvements in working conditions: the shops were heated and ventilated, and had lunchrooms, indoor toilets, playing fields and a library. By 1916, the Angus shops employed a workforce of more than 6,000. The shops were closed as a railway facility in 1992; the large property is currently in transition and part of it has been converted to commercial space.

Richard Bladworth Angus, 1911.
Photograph by William Notman & Son.

Purchase from Associated Screen News Ltd., McCord Museum, II-185736

Duncan McIntyre

Duncan McIntyre (born in Callander, Scotland, in 1834; died in Montreal in 1894) is sometimes known as Canada's "Napoleon of finance."

Duncan McIntyre came to Canada with his parents in 1849 and later joined a family wholesale business in Montreal. He remained with the firm all his life and made his fortune, riding out the depression of the mid-1850s with the toughness, stubbornness and practicality typical of the Montreal Scots merchants of the time.

In the early 1860s, McIntyre decided to improve customer service by investing in two railways, mainly in the Canada Central Railway. In 1878, he became Vice-President of the new Canadian Pacific Railway. Before the line was completed, however, a fierce argument over financing with President George Stephen prompted him to sell all his shares to Stephen and Donald Smith. An American railwayman, William Cornelius Van Horne, took his place as vice-president. When he died, McIntyre was considered one of the five richest men in Canada.

Duncan McIntyre was a founding member of the Caledonian Society and took part in the events held by the Scottish organization. He was president of the St. Andrew's Society, and naturally wore a kilt at the annual St. Andrew's Ball.

"The individual Gael was a stout, dark, young man, of low stature,
the ample folds of whose plaid added to the appearance of strength which his person exhibited.
The short kilt, or petticoat, showed his sinewy and clean made limbs; the goat-skin purse, flanked
by the usual defences, a dirk and steel-wrought pistol, hung before him; his bonnet had a short
feather, which indicated his claim to be treated as a *Duinhé-wassel*, or sort of gentleman;
a broadsword dangled by his side, a targe hung upon his shoulder,
and a long Spanish fowling piece occupied one of his hands."

—Walter Scott, *Waverly*, 1814

Duncan McIntyre, 1892.
Photograph by William Notman & Son, painted by George Horne Russell (1861-1933).

Gift of the Estate of Robert Snowball, McCord Museum, N-1981.207.21

The Scottish Baronial architectural style became very popular in Montreal in the latter half of the 19th century, not only for homes but also for public buildings like McGill University, the Saint-Louis du Mile End City Hall and Viger Station. It was patterned after 17th-century towered Scottish castles with their austere walls, corbelled battlements, crow-stepped gables and asymmetrically arranged crenellated turrets. There are still numerous examples of these buildings in many different parts of Montreal.

Duncan McIntyre's Scottish Baronial-style residence, Craigruie, was built in the 1880s and demolished in 1930.

Duncan McIntyre's house Craigruie,
McGregor Street (now Docteur-Penfield) and Drummond, Montreal, circa 1890.
Photograph by William Notman & Son.

Purchase from Associated Screen News Ltd., McCord Museum, VIEW-2547

John Young

John Young (1811-78) was the son of a cooper. He began trading in American goods, mainly rice and tobacco, when he arrived in Montreal in 1826 from his native Scotland. Young had made astute observations about shipping traffic and, influenced by the observations of Scottish economist Adam Smith, he saw the potential for Montreal to become the hub of a network stretching across Canada.

For most of his life Young proposed, defended and implemented ambitious projects to improve transportation infrastructures. His visionary qualities brought him to the attention of the political and financial élite. A free-trader and a progressive politician, he was a member of the Legislative Assembly in 1849 and voted for the Rebellion Losses Bill.

The ideas Young proposed and carried out while sitting on the Montreal Harbour Commission were probably the most remarkable of his many achievements. Until 1850, only ships under 600 tons and drawing less than 11 feet (slightly over 3 metres) could reach Montreal. Young reduced costly trans-shipping from Quebec to Montreal when he had a channel dredged to a depth of 27 1/2 feet (about 8.4 metres) so large transatlantic steamers could reach Montreal. He was also responsible for the building of modern wharves, eliminating the need to bring goods ashore in smaller boats.

In 1850, as Montreal's Chief Commissioner for Public Works, Young obtained a government lease for the exclusive use of waterpower generated at the St. Gabriel Lock on the Lachine Canal. This energy would run the first factories that set up along the banks of the Canal in 1853, including John Redpath's sugar refinery and, in 1854, the Goudie and Ogilvie's Glenora flour mill.

John Young was one of the first to suggest that the two shores of the St. Lawrence be linked by a permanent bridge. Every year, shipping between Canada and the British Empire was cut off by ice. Building the Victoria Bridge to carry a railway line across the River put an end to this obstacle to trade by giving businesses access to the port of Portland, Maine, which was open year-round.

A monument to John Young was erected in 1913 and it still stands in the Old Port of Montreal on de la Commune Street, in front of the Allan Building.

Victoria Bridge, 1854 (before the bridge was built).
Hand–coloured lithograph. Lithograph by S. Russel, printed by Day & Son.

Purchase from Christie, Mason and Woods, McCord Museum, M969.81

Monument to John Young, Montreal, 1913.
Photograph by William Notman & Son.

Purchase from Associated Screen News Ltd., McCord Museum, VIEW-4993.

The Photographers

The Notman Photographic Archives of the McCord Museum
comprise close to one million photos, over half of them taken by two Scots,
William Notman and Alexander Henderson. This is such an exceptional legacy
that it is difficult to find a single publication on the history of Montreal, Quebec or Canada
that does not contain at least one photo by these artists of light.

William Notman

William Notman (born in Paisley, Scotland, in 1826; died in Montreal in 1891) came from a typical middle-class Scottish family of the early 19th century, one that valued schooling, hard work and ambition. He arrived in Montreal in the mid-1850s and opened a photography studio in 1856.

Two years later, he won the contract to capture the construction of the Victoria Bridge with photographs. The box containing the portfolio of photographs that he gave to the Canadian government for presentation to the Prince of Wales at the opening ceremonies for the bridge was so impressive that it delighted even Queen Victoria, who proclaimed Notman "Photographer to the Queen."

By the mid-1860s, Notman's studio had 35 employees and artists who prepared sitters for portraits, coloured photos with oil or watercolour paints, and produced composite photos by arranging many smaller photos on the same background. Notman was known for his innovations, and the studio soon became so popular that he opened branches throughout Canada and the United States. By 1880 there were twenty Notman branches. Two years later, his son, William McFarlane, became a partner in William Notman & Son. On William McFarlane's death, his brother Charles Frederick took the reins until 1935, when the company was sold to Associated Screen News Ltd.

The Notman Photographic Archives at the McCord Museum holds the largest collection of the work of William Notman and his studio, comprising over 450,000 images.

William Notman, 1891.
Photograph on canvas by the Notman Studio, Boston, painted in oil by George Horne Russell (1861-1933)

Gift of Mrs. James Geoffrey Notman, McCord Museum, N-1975.4.5002

Alexander Henderson

Alexander Henderson (born in Scotland in 1831; died in Montreal in 1913) was the grandson of the Lord Provost of Edinburgh and the first President of the National Bank of Scotland, and son of a prosperous nursery owner. Henderson had every advantage one could wish to succeed in politics or finance. Yet when he arrived in Montreal in 1855, he chose to study photography. At first he was a serious amateur, but he opened a studio in 1866, in competition with his compatriot, advisor and friend, William Notman.

In 1870, by personal preference or because he wished to avoid this rivalry, he gave up portrait photography and concentrated on landscapes. He travelled from coast to coast, tirelessly capturing images of the country for the Intercolonial Railway, the Canadian Pacific Railway or simply for his own pleasure. After Henderson's death, his immense collection of glass negatives was stored in the basement of his home. Unfortunately, in the 1950s his grandson and only surviving relative consigned them all to the garbage. As a result, Alexander Henderson's work is known only from his prints. One of the largest collections of these prints is at the McCord Museum.

Alexander Henderson, 1897.
Photograph by William Notman & Son.

Purchase from Associated Screen News Ltd., McCord Museum, II-122466

Drawing water, Phillips Square, circa 1869. Photograph by Alexander Henderson (1831-1913).

Purchase from John L. Russell, McCord Museum, MP-0000.10.79

Sherbrooke Street in winter, 1896. Photograph by William Notman & Son.

Purchase from Associated Screen News Ltd., McCord Museum, VIEW-2801

Tobogganing, Mount Royal, circa 1870. Photograph by Alexander Henderson (1831-1913).

Gift from Miss E. Dorothy Benson, McCord Museum, MP-0000.1452.72

Montreal, from below Côte-des-Neiges toll gate, 1859.
Photograph by William Notman (1826-91).

Gift from James Geoffrey Notman, McCord Museum, N-0000.193.62.2

Ice cutting. Photograph by Alexander Henderson (1831-1913).

Gift from Miss E. Dorothy Benson, McCord Museum, MP-0000.1452.40

St. Urbain Street, 1860.
Photograph by William Notman (1826-91).

Purchase from Associated Screen News Ltd., McCord Museum, VIEW-7073.0

Frozen pigs, St. Anne's Market, circa 1870. Photograph by Alexander Henderson (1831-1913).

Gift from Stanley G. Triggs, McCord Museum, MP-0000.1828.82

Tanneries Village, St. Henry, 1859. Photograph by Alexander Henderson (1831-1913).

Purchase from John L. Russell, McCord Museum, MP-0000.10.95

(left) Master L.D. Ross, Montreal, 1865. Photograph by William Notman (1826-91).

Purchase from Associated Screen News Ltd., McCord Museum, I-15386

(right) Master Henry Ogg, Montreal, 1863. Photograph by William Notman (1826-91).

Purchase from Associated Screen News Ltd., McCord Museum, I-7936.1

(left) Miss Anderson, Montreal, 1914. Photograph by William Notman & Son.

Purchase from Associated Screen News Ltd., McCord Museum, II-202860;

(right) Master D. Craig, Montreal, 1875. Photograph by William Notman (1826-91).

Purchase from Associated Screen News Ltd., McCord Museum, II-20481

Conclusion

The Scots left their homeland in search of a better life. They made many significant and lasting contributions to the building of Montreal and Canada, and played significant roles in the business life and the institutions of Montreal. They also made their mark in politics, education, culture and the professions, and were prominent in the social life of the city. We still see their influence in the stones and mortar of Montreal's built heritage, streets and landmarks.

This book provides but a small glimpse into the lives of many generations of Montreal Scots. Some became entrepreneurs, both large and small. Only a small number became rich and famous and lived in the prestigious "Square Mile".

Others worked in trades and factories, as domestics and day labourers and were an active part of more modest neighbourhoods. They built churches, schools, businesses and social institutions, and maintained strong community ties and traditions.

The images and objects in the original exhibition and in this book only touch the surface of the rich diversity of the Scots of Montreal. They entice us to explore further this thread that runs so prominently through the fabric of Montreal's history.

Index of People and Institutions